The Art Of Negotiation

*Life is all about negotiation.
Learn how to win in life by
learning how to close a deal.*

Peter Oliver

THE ART OF NEGOTIATION
Copyright © 2016, 2017 by Concise Reads™

TABLE OF CONTENTS

INTRODUCTION

"In Business as in life, you don't get what you deserve, you get what you negotiate."
- Chester L. Karrass

Dr. Chester Karrass is a pioneer in business negotiation who researched and wrote extensively on the subject matter and who first developed the Effective Negotiating seminar in 1968. We will learn from him, as well as from Roger Fisher, Dale Carnegie and others what the elements and principles are of an artful and masterful negotiation. Some naysayers would say "I don't need to learn negotiating, I've been getting my way my whole life". That's not true anymore. With flatter organizations, working in teams, and working with people of different beliefs, culture, or values necessitates a different approach to getting what we want without losing it with the old tactics of stonewalling, walking out, or unwillingness to compromise.

We want a lot of things in life whether it is convincing our child to go to bed, our spouse to join us in our favorite activity, our boss to give us a better salary, our co-workers to buy into our project, or a competitor, supplier, or government official to help us increase revenue or decrease costs. We have to negotiate in all these events and we can lose that which we desire because we are unskilled at negotiation.

This book will walk us through initial simple two party negotiations to multi-party negotiations, disputes, and mediation. These are basic principles taught in business school, in management seminars, and in leadership programs. Many of the principles are derived from countless books on the subject matter that were prolific in the 1980s and 1990s and some as far back as the turn of the 20th century. You should be able to read through this in one day, but make sure to underline or highlight the sections that you want to come back to, and come back to them often. These principles need to be practiced in order to become part of your routine. So practice, practice, practice...starting with your closest friends and family and then extending your practice into the business world.

This book focuses largely on the compromising and collaborating negotiation styles by going through multiple principled techniques in different negotiation scenarios. Because the type of deals vary as much as our personalities are varied, you are to learn all the techniques cold and depending on the type of deal you are faced with--you will employ one or more of these techniques to your advantage. This concise read also contains a bonus section on body language. Learn that and practice it in your everyday life because a deal is not taking place only when you plan for it, but a deal can take place during any conversation you engage in. That is why this book is very special. Again, remember to practice, practice, practice as these techniques will be most useful to you when they become second nature.

SIMPLE TWO-PARTY NEGOTIATIONS

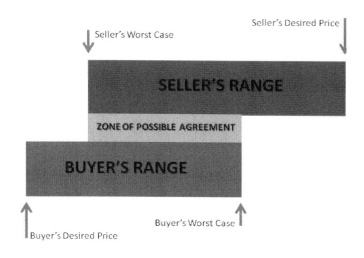

Zone of Possible Agreement (ZONA)

In simple two-party negotiations there is a bargaining zone where the target for each party in the negotiation is to fall beyond the 50% line in their bargaining zone. Each party's bargaining zone has a reservation or bottom where they are not willing to accept a deal below that. There is also a fair settlement in the bargaining zone with anything above that providing surplus benefit. Start thinking of a negotiation as finding agreement in the ZONA while keeping in mind that some negotiations can have a very narrow ZONA. We will come back to this concept when we talk of BATNA.

Negotiation Styles

The Thomas-Kilmann Conflict Mode Instrument (TKI) was developed by Kenneth W. Thomas and Ralph H. Kilmann in the early 1970s. The model is based on an earlier model of management styles proposed by Robert Blake and Jane Mouton in the 1960s.

The TKI model is a five-category scheme for classifying interpersonal conflict-handling behavior. It has been validated by several research studies since it was first developed. The five negotiation styles are described in relation to the different desires to be **assertive** (concern for self) vs. **cooperative** (concern for others). The 5 negotiation styles (assertive, cooperative) are:

1. **Avoiding** (low assertiveness, low cooperativeness): avoid negotiation

2. **Accommodating** (low assertiveness, high cooperativeness): yield negotiation

3. **Compromising** (middle assertiveness, middle cooperativeness): find middle ground

4. **Competing** (high assertiveness and low cooperativeness): win or lose but never settle

5. **Collaborating** (high assertiveness, high cooperativeness): win-win situation

People who use a **competing** strategy enjoy conflict and can take extreme positions that make them lose many deals that could have been made. The problem with **collaboration** is that it requires a high investment of time to reach the perfect 'win, win' situation and less likely to reach a fair middle ground with a competing personality.

On the other hand the **compromising** position (the middle ground) is more likely to reach a fair outcome with the majority of conflict resolution strategies. This doesn't mean that there couldn't be more strategies or even blended strategies. The takeaway is to identify which strategy you used before reading this book, and to start buying into the evidence that the **compromising** strategy is the best one for most negotiations except for complex problems.

Complex problems that can afford to take a very long time to reach resolution benefit most from **collaboration** (think partnership) in order to yield a better outcome.

Compromising strategy is not about giving in or giving up and this will be more thoroughly explained as we move through this book. Dr. Chester Karrass reminds us that compromise is to "never give a concession without obtaining one in return."

Hard & Soft Bargainers

Traditionally the basic types of negotiators were the hard and soft bargainers likened to the competing and the accommodating negotiation styles. The idiom "you drive a hard bargain" was meant as a complement after accepting a deal. Yet while some are hard bargainers and other are told that hard bargaining is the best strategy, it turns out their strategies often fail, except when planned on soft bargainers. A soft bargainer wishes to maintain the relationship and would make concessions if he thought the relationship was at jeopardy. These are bargainers whom the Harvard Negotiation Project has identified as people who do not separate *the people from the problem*. It's actually kind of sad to watch, but it happens all the time and seasoned hard bargainers can spot a soft one a mile away. Parents can be soft bargainers, so can spouses, and employees. A hard bargainer would use tactics such as threatening to walk out on a negotiation, putting pressure by insisting that this is their final offer and they don't care if a deal is made or not.

They enjoy the thrill and chaos associated with the risk of losing the deal, because winning it would make it *feel* worth so much more than it really is. Unfortunately, hard bargainers lose more often than not because not everyone is a soft bargainer, and then they tell themselves that the deal wasn't worth it anyway and never count the number of lost deals to prove that there should be a better way.

There is a better way. The principled negotiator, which we will cover next in the book, uses a standard to counter positions taken by hard bargainers such as refusal to negotiate, extreme demands, escalating demands, or lock-in tactics (where the other party forces themselves into only one outcome, either to make a specific deal or to lose the deal completely).

Principled Negotiation

This is a negotiation method taught as part of the Harvard Program On Negotiation (PON) first developed in 1983 by Roger Fisher, William Ury, and Bruce Patton. It is also the subject matter of a three decade old book, *Getting To Yes: Negotiating Agreement Without Giving In,* which is one of the longest running best sellers in paperback business books. The premise is that we are all used to what is known as **positional** negotiations, where we decide to take a position or outcome in a negotiation and then fight tooth and nail to hold on to that position. The more we fight for that position, the less willing we are to accept any alternative.

This type of negotiating can damage relationships and does not lead to a win-win situation. Relationships are important, and we never know when a deal will need to be re-negotiated or a new deal negotiated in the future. The opposite extreme of positional negotiations is to concede every position in order to preserve the relationship. The principled negotiation approach is a **middle approach** that is "hard on the merits (but) soft on the people" according to Fisher, Ury, and Patton.

It is based on the following principles:

1. Separate **People** from the **Problem**: People problems are broken down into <u>perception</u>, <u>emotion</u>, and <u>communication</u>. First of all,

make sure you don't include the people in the problem. That means that the problem is never someone's mistake, oversight, or deliberate action. It is just a problem, and you are trying to reach a happy outcome *together*. Thus it makes it important to consider how you phrase the problem. Put yourself in their shoes. Don't blame them. Make sure you consider their values. Factor in <u>emotions</u> such as: the **need for autonomy** (the ability to choose a decision), **appreciation** (to be recognized for the working elements of the problem), **affiliation** (desire to belong to a group), **role** (the desire to have a purpose), and **status** (the desire to be recognized). In terms of communication, it is a 2-way street. Make sure not to begin negotiations by stating the problem, don't talk about them rather talk about your interests, and make sure to really listen and hear their interests and opinion. Of course, all this consideration can be avoided if there is already a healthy relationship in place. That's why negotiation actually starts long before the negotiation in the form of <u>relationship building</u>--making sure to voice and hear concerns long before sitting down to make a deal. This takes the people out of the problem when the time comes to negotiate.

2.   Focus on the **Interests**, Not Positions: Always focus on your interests and make sure you have more than one. At the same time, accept that the other party can have multiple interests and actively engage them to find out what those are. The summary

position is that you are negotiating on interests not on positions. You must *explicitly* state some or all of your interests so the other party can factor them in. Don't take a position, but rather encourage a collaborative coming to a mutually beneficial position. For example, if you are a parent worried that cars are driving too fast in your neighborhood. Don't go demanding a stop sign to your local government official. Instead go and explain the problem from the perspective of what your interests are such as a safer neighborhood for your children. The solution may end up not involving a stop sign and instead involve an even more effective solution at ensuring the safety of the neighborhood children.

3.   Invent on **Options** for Mutual Gain: This is straightforward. Before stepping into the negotiation, come up with all the possible solutions or outcomes that would result in a win-win. This assumes you have a good estimate of the other party's interests in order to factor them in. You don't pick the best option, you just come up with multiple possible options that both you and the other party would agree on. This has a tremendous effect on allowing **you** to come to an agreement faster.

4.   Insist on Using **Objective Criteria:** This is an important concept and like point (3) also requires preparation prior to negotiation. Any position discussed during negotiation should have some form of logical deduction from an acceptable standard or 'fair' benchmark. If you are negotiating the price of a home, you should factor in how much it sold previously, as well as inflation, taxes, modifications, or

how much a comparable home sold for. If the other party takes a position, especially an extreme one such as insisting on paying $200,000 for a $300,000 home, then insist on using objective criteria and ask them how they came to that number. **There is no counterargument to using objective criteria**. If the other party insists on "that's what I want to pay! I don't care about what's fair!' then obviously, you will have to revisit the negotiation at another date when both parties are willing to negotiate using objective criteria. There is a different scenario when the other party changes its position after the deal was done. This is known as *bad faith negotiation* and we'll learn more in the next section.

Knowing your BATNA: Before going into a negotiation we should come up with the **Best Alternative To a Negotiated Agreement**. This frames your absolute bottom or reserve position in a negotiation. The better your BATNA the more comfortable you are to negotiate for something better. You can apply BATNA to empower you by securing multiple job offer before walking into a salary negotiation. Similarly, it is better to ask for multiple offers from suppliers or contractors before going into any negotiation with any one of them. The concept of BATNA does not only applies to yourself and that is the beauty of BATNA. You should also apply it to the other party in the negotiation. Do they have a best alternative to a negotiated agreement? What is it? If it is a really good BATNA, is there a way to make their BATNA less of a good option? (ethically of course). Thus as part of your pre-planning for a negotiation, know you BATNA in case a deal cannot be made, know your reservation price, also known as <u>least acceptable solution (LAS)</u>, and the best possible offer within the ZONA or your target offer, also known as <u>maximum supportable solution (MSS)</u>.

Bad Faith Negotiation

Sometimes despite preparing for a negotiation, taking the people out of the problem, negotiating on interests not positions, and inventing multiple options, the other party could pretend to negotiate, even come to some settlement but have no intention to actually follow through. This is considered a bad faith negotiation. Three ways this is possible is by providing **false facts** to build a case, by **not having the appropriate authority** to make a deal, and by **not having the right character** or intention to follow through. The best way to prepare for a bad faith negotiation is to know who you are negotiating with and have prepared the standard with which the possible outcomes can be compared to.

Imagine you are trying to buy a car from a used car salesman. You go back and forth on what you can afford, and what he can do for you. Then finally when he thinks he got you to as low as he can possibly get you in terms of price, he says that he doesn't actually have the authority to finalize the deal and he'll just step in and check with his manager. Then he comes back and takes away one of the things he promised you. In this type of negotiation, it's great to itemize the cost of every item that goes into a car as you are negotiating and have a reference to compare that price to. Then if the salesman or any other party in a similar negotiation tells you they don't have the authority to make a deal, then you should let them know that you will likely change your position by the time they comes back and start the negotiation process again from the first item on the list when they come back or with their manager. On that point be aware that salespeople are trained to feign that they've reached their bottom, it's a hard bargaining tactic employing body language with a sharp exhale, eyes wondering as if they are undergoing heavy computational reasoning, or the withdrawn lips with a "I don't know if that would work…" expression on their face.

Again, separate the people from the problem, and focus on your interest and on using some fair standard in the negotiation. Their BATNA is actually pretty weak because they depend on the commissions for a salary and your BATNA is a similar car on another lot (but maybe with a different color) or an extra day without a car. Remember to come prepared with a reservation price (absolute maximum price), a researched BATNA, a fair standard to compare to, and different options/agreements you are willing to accept for the next time you'll be shopping for used cars.

Watch this video to see examples of conducting research to know one's BANTA, making a first offer at the last dealership visited, anchoring the price with small incremental changes, and lastly a very important lesson of **separating people from the problem**. <https://youtu.be/UpEsmEaJcJo>. This video shows a buyer who visited multiple car dealerships to see what offers they would get for a specific type of used vehicle. The buyer incorrectly calls their negotiation skills as 'haggling', but aside from some gimmicks like walking out of the lot or playing good cop/bad cop, their offer was based on researching their options and knowing their reservation price ahead of the deal which equipped them with the confidence to negotiate and to know when to accept or decline a final offer.

Make The First Offer

If the other negotiator is known to negotiate based on interests as in the principled negotiation then it won't matter who makes the first offer because you will <u>anchor</u> the positions to some standard. However, if you are going in blind and don't know what type of negotiator they are, it's best to make the first offer. Non-principled negotiators take extreme positions as far away from their BATNA as they think you would assume is reasonable. The problem there is that they set anchor at such an extreme that it would take a lot of negotiating to move them to something more realistic. To avoid multiple offers and counteroffers, it is better to make the first offer and anchor the offer to some fair standard. Negotiation research has shown that more often than not, those who make the first offer tend to get a final offer closer to what they want. When you lose the chance to make the first offer and the first offer is exactly what you wanted, make sure to ask for additional concessions before accepting because accepting right away gives the other party a feeling of regret, that they somehow 'left money on the table', and we don't want that because we want a good relationship for the next negotiation or even just to see this one through. If the first offer is extreme, then continue negotiated using the principled negotiator approach. Repeat to yourself that a first offer **anchors** the negotiation.

INTEGRATIVE NEGOTIATIONS

Distributive Vs. Integrative Negotiation

In negotiation science, if you assume the pie is fixed then you have to participate in distributive negotiation where you negotiate for a share of the pie. On the other hand, if you assume the pie can grow with cooperation then you are participating in integrative negotiation. This is also called interest-based bargaining or win-win situations. So is the pie always fixed or can it be expanded? There are many situations when the pie is fixed and cooperating to find a middle ground through *compromise* is the best solution. Other time, one or both parties could come up with creative ways to increase the pie so that neither has to compromise and instead can collaborate. These win-win situations are ideal but can often take time to develop, negotiate, and execute. Again, finding these creative solutions is an interest-based bargain and implies talking about and learning what the interests of both parties are. Remember leading with interests rather than a final outcome will help you close the deal.

From Distributive To Integrative

To try to move from a distributive to an integrative negotiation requires you be creative and find value. The following are the three steps required to move the conversation from distributive to an integrative negotiation:

1. Build Trust

2. Ask the right questions
3. Make equivalent simultaneous offers

Build Trust

Trust is important in negotiation because it prevents emotions from taking over and a positional negotiation dominating. It also allows for more open exchange of interests which will allow the negotiations to reach more of the middle region of ZONA if the pie is fixed or reach new creative solutions if the pie can be expanded. There are a few basic assumptions that are required before trust is established. These assumptions are **credibility** and **reliability** which require prior knowledge of the person you are negotiating with (as well as your reputation). Additionally **intimacy and trustworthiness** (listening, or sharing of personal information) are important during the negotiation and are important qualities in networking as well. However, with regards to business negotiation, **reliability** is the most important to the foundation of building trust. It behooves you to prove you are reliable leading up to the negotiation by sending any required documents on time, showing up on time, not rescheduling negotiations, and coming ready to negotiate. The old tactics of delaying the negotiation, walking out, and seeming unavailable only fuel positional negotiating and will likely end a deal. Think of a time when you agreed on a deal but the other party took too long to make the offer official. For some it almost tempted them to re-negotiate, for others it often does. After establishing reliability, it is important to establish trust. It may seem counterintuitive but to show trustworthiness you have to focus on the needs and interests of the other person instead of your needs. In Game theory, the most successful outcome is when one partner matches exactly what the other partner chooses only if they know what the other wants. We discuss some aspects of how body language plays a role in building trust in the last section, and we've also previously covered Dale Carnegie's principles to get someone to like you and trust in you in the Concise Reads book **Leadership Principles**.

Here is a summary of those principles as a reminder:

1. Don't criticize, condemn or complain.

2. Give honest, sincere appreciation.

3. Arouse in the other person an eager want.

4. Become genuinely interested in other people.

[Carnegie emphasized being genuine multiple times because it affects your body language so much that it takes away any feeling of being false or fake in your enthusiasm.]

5. Smile.

6. Remember that a person's name is to that person the most important sound in any language.

7. Be a good listener. Encourage others to talk about themselves.

8. Talk in terms of the other person's interest.

[This is very important during negotiation. Keep this in mind always.]

9. Make the other person feel important - and do so sincerely.

10. The only way to get the best of an argument is to avoid it.

Ask The Right Questions

Distributive negotiation as we learned refers to a fixed pie, while integrative negotiation refers to an expanded pie where everybody wins. Some negotiations are inherently distributive like when haggling over price with a street vendor. That is because price is the only issue on the table. However there are many issues that can be uncovered, thereby expanding the fixed pie.

Asking the right questions is important to understand the other person's interests and uncover their BATNA. Only then can you find creative terms to the negotiation that would find agreement with both parties. The goal of asking questions is to move from a debate to a discussion. Imagine you find an expert in a subject matter and try to negotiate profit sharing for a nationwide seminar series. The expert would argue that since the content of the seminar series depends on their expertise, that they are entitled to a larger share of the profits. On the other hand, since you are providing the capital, marketing, and promotion you should have a larger share of the profits. Arguing on those terms will never move the negotiation forward. Instead, if the expert asked you what can he do to de-risk your investment, and you asked the expert what he would need to do to appeal to a larger audience and what does he need to meet his expectations, then the terms of the negotiation just expanded considerably. The type of questions one should be asking are circular or open-ended. They don't have a predetermined response. Instead they aim to **uncover** the basis of each other's position as well as any potential terms on which to negotiate on. Asking the expert what dollar value he would put on his expertise is a <u>leading question</u>, one that from the start implies you think his or her dollar value will never command a higher share of the profits. Leading questions will only make the expert take a defensive stance, bringing you back to a debate instead of a discussion. Do not ask leading questions in a negotiation.

The Story of the Local Baker: There once was a local baker whose experience in negotiation was a lesson for many students of the art. Business was declining for the baker and he even thought of closing his bakery at the end of the year until a young prince smelled the delicious aroma of freshly baked dough. The prince wanted to hire the baker to bake goods for this weekend's party at the royal palace. The prince wanted to impress the king by bargaining for a good deal. The prince asked for a price that was just above cost and significantly below what the baker would typically sell his goods for. The baker realizing that his BATNA was to close down his bakery within a year, decided to see how else he could make the terms more favorable. He asked the prince "What type of event is this? Do you hold events often where you would need baked goods?" The prince told him that this weekend's event was to celebrate spring, and that he always holds weekly events to celebrate people and nature. The Baker then told him that the price the prince is asking for would leave very little profit for him, but if he were to allow the Baker to sell additional special treats at the party like chocolate at the typical retail price, then he would be happy to bake goods every weekend for the young prince. The prince elated that he got a bargain, happily accepted. The Baker having secured a new source of consistent income happily rejoiced. The morale of this story is to ask questions to uncover terms that make a negotiation favorable for both parties.

Multiple Equivalent Simultaneous Offers (MESOs)

This strategy is to focus your attention on the middle offer. Think Goldilocks and the three bears. She didn't like the extremes of temperature in the porridge or the hardness of the bed. Instead she preferred the middle choice. It is useful to uncover terms and move to an integrative negotiation, but it is an especially effective strategy when negotiating with a team because of their different preferences, interest, and needs. Imagine you offer another party the choice between a fast and expensive car or a slow and affordable car. If they lean more towards the slow and affordable car, you automatically uncover the preference for an affordable car over a fast one, and can then give them a third option of an even slower but very affordable car. MESOs help uncover preferences or additional terms to negotiate on without using open ended questions or in addition to a constructive discussion.

Alternatively, MESOs can be used to demonstrate flexibility and willingness to be agreeable with multiple options making the other party feel that they have a choice, when all choices work equally well for you. MESOs require a lot of pre negotiation planning but can be used in the beginning, middle, or end of negotiation to uncover preference, reset the anchor, and continue to move towards terms that are agreeable to both parties. The important planning aspect of this negotiation technique is to set up a scoring system for all the different issues or terms so that if the other party's preferences overlap between offers, you can quickly calculate whether the cherry picked offer is still acceptable for you. The obvious use case for this type of negotiation is when there are many issues, many terms, or many parties to negotiate. If this use case applies to you, then be sure to write out all the possible combination of terms that you would accept and rank them according to which is most profitable for you and which is likely most profitable for the person or team you are negotiating with. Unlike in single offers where you lead with your interest, in this scenario you don't divulge all your interests except for a few. You will find that while the other party thinks you are making a concession, you are actually agreeing to your 4th or 5th interest.

MORE COMPLEX NEGOTIATIONS

Building Contingency

Sometimes a deal involves risks. Adding contingencies to the terms of a deal can help enforce the terms, manage future disagreements, and reduce chances for litigation. You may have noticed that real estate owners of apartment rentals are beginning to de-risk against future disasters by requiring tenants purchase renters insurance for damage to their property, liability insurance for damage to their person, and sometimes even crime insurance for theft of tenant's property. Homeowners now build in a contingency bonus payment if the contractors were to finish their work before the deadline and a penalty if the work were to exceed the deadline. If in this situation a contractor refuses to sign with that contingency, then ask them why, and the answer might be that there is a chance the project will become overdue. In this case, armed with new information, it is time to renegotiate the final price to reflect the increased uncertainty of the delivery date. Complex negotiations involve risk, and understanding the risks helps you come to a more aggregable final offer. In the case of buyer and contractor, the contractor has all the information regarding risk and this leads to asymmetry of information. That is why contingencies matter.

Additionally, contingencies help to solve contract breaches without the need for additional negotiations. If a contingency is placed to address each potential breach, then by signing a contract, the law becomes pretty black and white, and this avoids legal fees.

Although an annoying practice for renters, using the same landlord tenant lease example, while the lease is filled with multiple ways to breach the contract and multiple different penalties associated with breaching the contract, it also adds an additional term to the contract that if there are any legal fees due, they would be automatically owed by the tenant in the event that it is due to an issue that the landlord was not able to think of and list at the time of the contract. The lease example is a little unfair because the tenant typically has little buying power to negotiate the terms--that's why we rely on the government to protect our fair housing rights in markets where the seller has no incentive to negotiate. There is a valuable lesson from carefully reading a lease agreement. It will show you how much landlords have de-risked their investment and future liability through the use of contingencies in contracts. In other situations where both parties have more to gain, contingencies help reduce risk, increase incentives to complete the deal, and allow the contract to solve instances of disagreement or breach of contract. The contingencies in this case actually help get a deal closed by assuring both parties of payment or non-payment in the event of a risk occurrence.

Perspective Taking

The old adage of withholding judgment until you've walked a mile in someone else's shoes is also true during negotiations. Don't be offended of an extreme first offer, assuming you didn't have the chance to make it yourself and anchor the terms of the negotiation. We learned to always try to uncover additional terms and preferences through asking questions or by using MESOs. One more tool to uncover interests and motivations is perspective taking. Imagine a famous chef suddenly wants to sell their restaurant at the highest bid offer. It is time to try and understand why. Are they nearing retirement? Do they have teenagers going to college, and they need to pay their tuition? Maybe your company has secured bargain deals for retirement vacations or your company offers a college scholarship specifically to children of culinary experts. You could these additional terms to the deal to land at a more attractive offer for both parties. Using perspective taking will allow you to uncover even more potential points of negotiation, especially when each party's ZONA never overlaps based on existing terms such as a low bid and a high reservation price. Maybe the retirement home requires a fixed deposit that can only be reached with a high bid but by offering a retirement home discount that your company already has negotiated for it's own employees then you can settle on a more reasonable price point.

Rebuilding Trust

In a situation where trust was lost because of an argument, an accidental insensitivity, or for any reason, the most important building block to bring the other party back to the negotiation table is to build trust again. This begins by using Dale Carnegie's lessons of getting people to like you by learning everything you can about them and their business, and then shifting the conversation to what they want and need. Hold your demands until the end of the negotiation. After you have barely rekindled the trust by showing gratitude for the past relationship and concern for their concerns, the next step is to make what is called in the industry a **unilateral concession**. This has been shown many times to regain trust. However, the order of events is important. If the unilateral concession was made without first meeting with the other party and listening to their concerns, it would appear as just a cheap move to close a deal. After the unilateral concession, you then need to explicitly state all the concessions you've made, and all the considerations you are willing to make. Often we assume people remember everything we've done for them, but they don't. Reminding them of all the concessions you made reminds them of your effort in this negotiation and because of **Adam's Equity Theory** that we learned in the **Leadership Principles** Concise Read, we know that if the concessions are unequal, that the other party will expect that it is their turn to make a concession. This is when you finally explicitly state your demands but more so explain your demand and what they are motivated by. Now the negotiation should be back to before the point it fell apart.

AFTER THE DEAL: DISPUTES AND MEDIATION

Legal Aspect of Negotiations: In cases of fraudulent statements, the plaintiff would have to prove that the speaker *knowingly* misrepresented a material fact that has caused *damage*. Of note, misrepresentation also includes knowingly omitting to state a material fact that has caused damage. There are good cases from history to illustrate this point:

1. **Leonard V Pepsico, Inc. 88 F. Supp. 2d 116, (S.D.N.Y. 1999), aff'd 210 F.3d 88 (2d Cir. 2000):** Pepsico had a promotions ad and included a Jet (for 7 million points). Leonard thought they were serious and sued for breach of contract when he didn't get the Jet. Summary judgement was for Pepsico and the appeals court agreed that the Harrier Fighter Jet was not an offer and no reasonable person would assume that was an offer. In this case, there was no misrepresentation.

2. **Lucy V Zehmer, 196 Va. 493; 84 S.E.2d 516 (1954):** Defendant A.H. Zehmer and his wife owned 471.6 acres in Virginia (the 'Ferguson Farm'). Plaintiff W.O. Lucy had expressed interest in buying the farm for many years, constantly bothering Zehmer to sell it. One day, Lucy walked into Zehmer's restaurant with a bottle of whisky and they both got inebriated. Lucy kept badgering Zehmer again about selling his land. Zehmer thought he would plan a joke on Lucy and pretend to sell

him the land. He went so far as to write ""We hereby agree to sell to W. O. Lucy the Ferguson Farm complete for $50,000.00, title satisfactory to buyer" on the back of a restaurant check. Because Zehmer's intent NOT to sell was not obvious, Lucy ended up suing and getting the Zehmer couple to honor the contract.

When it comes to what we have learned, a BATNA is material fact and false statements regarding your BATNA is subject to litigation. On the other hand, false statements regarding your reservation price is not subject to litigation nor should you ever disclose your reservation price. There are two aspects to a fraudulent statement and which one can be liable from. The first is 'knowing'. If one knows they are misrepresenting material facts, then they committed fraud. Also, if they go out of their way to be ignorant of material fact they are liable due to reckless statements. For example, an owner selling his company believes that the company is still in debt since he last looked at statements 6 months ago but deliberately does not look at any recent financial statements prior to a negotiation to avoid having to admit to any debt. The second aspect of a fraudulent statement is the misrepresentation causes damage to the victim who relies on it. For example, if a seller only gives partial information saying for example that they received 5 stars on Yelp but fail to disclose that Google Reviews has far more reviewers with an average review of 2 stars, then the seller is liable. Similarly, if the seller or buyer have additional information that very likely would prevent the deal from taking place but decide to withhold the information, they will be liable. On the other hand if a promise is made to appear as fact such that any reasonable party would assume it is fact, then the party making the promise is held liable if they decide not to deliver on that promise in post settlement. The short of it is not to make empty promises, false representations, or withhold information that could cause damage to the other party following agreement. Similarly, be sure to add contingencies in the event any fraud has taken place to avoid legal fees and allow the contract to pre-decide the penalty for misrepresentation.

BODY LANGUAGE IN NEGOTIATIONS

Because Negotiation involves elements of trust as well as instances of withholding information, Body language can serve both to help and hinder your negotiation goals. By understanding the basics of body language, you will be better prepared to examine the environment and use nonverbal cues to help with your strategy.

- **Non-Verbal Anchoring:** similar to anchoring the negotiation terms by making the first offer, one can anchor the negotiation non-verbally by building trust through a positive first impression (eye contact, positive gesture/greeting, and enthusiasm) and by leveling the playing field of a powerful negotiator by removing their personal space. For example, make sure to sit at the head of the table, or to invite the powerful negotiator to your office to sit in a less comfortable chair.

- Incongruity of verbal language and nonverbal body language:
  - **Nervous Laugh:** When this happens, ask for more information as they are having a hard time keeping the information hidden hence the nervous laugh.
  - **Clenched fists or folded arms:** This shows frustration and likely that the negotiator will take a positional strategy. It is time to improve the

relationship to bring the negotiator back to negotiating based on compromise and not position. To do this, you need to convey receptivity.

- o **Jaw muscles clenched and wondering eyes:** This is a tell-tale sign that the negotiator is not interested in coming up with creative ways to reach a compromise. Instead it is a sign that they have come with one premeditated goal and they are nervous that you may have figured it out. Even if you did, the goal will be to put them at ease by verbally stating that you are willing to make concessions if they are as well in order to reach agreement. Concessions seem more fair when they are two-sided as far as the other party is concerned.

- **Conveying Receptivity:**
  - o Smiling and Eye Contact: smiling and making eye contact gives the hint that you are interested in getting to know the person rather than just trying to hurry to a deal. This puts the other party at ease and prevents them from feeling that you somehow don't care whether they get something out of the negotiation or not.
  - o **Open hands:** One way to show you are open to negotiating is to keep your hands open, not clenched, by your side, on your hip, or on your lap. If

you have a nervous habit of rubbing your neck, running your hand through your hair, or talking with your hands, you run the risk of coming off as untrustworthy.

- o **Face the other party:** negotiators can lose trust which is the basis for concessions and ultimately reaching agreement by positioning their legs, feet, or body away from the other party. In short, if you look like you're in a hurry to leave, then the deal could fall through. If you're wearing a hat, take it off. If you're leaning back in your chair, lean forward, and if your legs are crossed or your feet are pointing away then uncross your legs and point your feet towards the other party. Being openly engaged will not only serve you well during negotiations, but will also convey receptivity in your relationships with your co-workers and with your boss.

- **Mirroring:**
  - o This can be both verbal and nonverbal. For whatever reason, and we don't have to get into it, people trust other people who 'seem similar' to them in both verbal and nonverbal communication. If your negotiation is over lunch, and the other party orders a beer, don't order a glass of wine. Similarly, if the other party takes off

their jacket, you should do the same, if only for the purpose of building trust. In terms of verbal mirroring, if the other party uses an antiquated expression or even uses it in the wrong context, don't correct them. Instead repeat the same expression or misused idiom and you will reinforce the idea that they aren't buying or trading from a stranger but rather someone who is similar enough to be considered part of the same social tribe. Technically, in psychology, mirroring is an unconscious activation of the mirror neurons compared to conscious imitation, but the more you practice, the more likely you will form a habit of mirroring and it won't appear as imitation.

CONCLUSION

The art of negotiation is an art because of the diversity of situation and people that one encounters during a negotiation. The art is based on fundamental scientific principles of psychology and from years of experience by some of the best negotiators.

Negotiation exits because the world does not think exactly the way we do nor are they incentivized to give us what we want. Negotiation is an essential skill, honed with time, that can get you closer to everything you want in life--one deal at a time. I hope you take the understanding gained from this Concise Read and apply it to both your career and your personal life.